A LIFE SHARED

Edited by

Heather Killingray

First published in Great Britain in 2000 by
POETRY NOW
Remus House,
Coltsfoot Drive,
Woodston,
Peterborough, PE2 9JX
Telephone (01733) 898101
Fax (01733) 313524

HB ISBN 0 75430 967 3
SB ISBN 0 75430 968 1

FOREWORD

Although we are a nation of poets we are accused of not reading poetry, or buying poetry books. After many years of listening to the incessant gripes of poetry publishers, I can only assume that the books they publish, in general, are books that most people do not want to read.

Poetry should not be obscure, introverted, and as cryptic as a crossword puzzle: it is the poet's duty to reach out and embrace the world.

The world owes the poet nothing and we should not be expected to dig and delve into a rambling discourse searching for some inner meaning.

The reason we write poetry (and almost all of us do) is because we want to communicate: an ideal; an idea; or a specific feeling. Poetry is as essential in communication, as a letter; a radio; a telephone, and the main criterion for selecting the poems in this anthology is very simple: they communicate.

CONTENTS

BROTHERS

Through childhood memories I delve
And reminisce when I was twelve
    A corner shop - the family Woods
    Who sold varieties of goods
And Bess and Nuck resided there
With Alan - elder son and heir
    On him I had a schoolgirl crush
    The sight of him would make me blush
But he was fourteen - had an eye
For older girls who weren't so shy!
    Yet we were friends, and we would talk
    He said - take Geoffrey for a walk
His baby brother - five weeks old
A tiny bundle - good as gold
    Maternal instincts rose in me
    My 'first born' child he came to be
I had my son, my joy, my pride
And so when I became a bride
    I wanted daughters - I confessed
    With two of them I was well-blessed

Geoff has two children of his own
Yet he 'minds' me, for I'm alone
    Our roles reversed by fate somehow
    My life has turned full circle now
I love him and his family -
He cares for me - it's plain to see
    And now, just like a dream come true
    His brother Alan loves me too!
Should we be wed - if that's the plan
Then Geoff will make a fine best man!

Arlene Skerratt

A MOTHER'S LOVE

My tiny miracle is born.
Safe, warm and cosy.
My precious, perfect child.
I gaze down upon my sleeping baby,
With such love and contentment.
I am so proud to be your mum.
I will watch you grow and flourish.
We shall have such a special bond.
We will be here for one another
Always caring, always strong.

Edwina Ann Kernot

MY DAD

My dad is mad
He makes me quite glad
He gets me up in the morning
While I'm still yawning
He makes me some coffee
While he eats all the toffee
My dad is mad!

My dad is mad
He makes me quite sad
He sends me to school
While he plays pool
Isn't he cruel
That's why my dad makes me sad!

My dad is mad
He makes me quite bad
I do doodles
And eat all his noodles
While he plays with my dog, Woodles
That's why my dad makes me mad!

He's really quite funny
And makes everything sunny
That's why I love my dad!

Hayley Oldfield (9)

LAST LOVE

*(This was written in memory of a dear friend who died of MS
and her feelings for her gentle husband)*

I loiter awhile
trapped inside my useless frame.
Unable to speak,
or whisper your precious name;
our eyes meet
as you carry me to our marriage bed,
such tenderness
as your lips caress my fevered head.
You lay me down
touch my cheek and wipe away my tears;
In your eyes, reflections,
memories of all our yesteryears . . .
The passions,
the love we shared, the happiness, the sadness,
the good times
the short golden years of gladness.
In my mind's eye
I see the credits rolling, I am near 'The end'
my love . . .
My last love . . . My final dearest friend . . .

Valerie McKinley

MY SON

A daughter's a daughter all her life
A son's only a son till he takes a wife
This is an old saying handed down through the years
For most of us mothers it brings many fears

My son was the best friend I ever had
He took the place of his runaway dad
He helped me keep my daughter in tow
And protected us both, and loved us so

So when the day came he decided to wed
I thought my life would be empty and dead
But this didn't happen, he didn't desert me
He'd call every night for us both to see

He was a pillar of strength to us
And he'd do anything without any fuss
There was no falling out with sister and brother
And this is a thank you from your loving mother

E A Lilley

ZUZKA

Happy, warm and bright,
Playfully patient, friendly and funny,
A pleasure to meet, a pleasure to know,
A gem among children I'd say.
Some moments of madness, sadness and tears,
But mostly smiles and laughter are near.
Growing and learning, learning and growing.
Each day a fresh new adventure to play.
Be happy world, Zuzka is on her way.

Alan Harrison

A FRIEND INDEED

In a troubled world I can recall
A special pal who could cope with all
On her I always would depend
My faithful mentor - my best friend
Other friends would come and go
But this dear one I always know
Would be there for me, good and kind
To soothe my ills and ease my mind
On days when skies bore clouds of grey
She'd swiftly sweep them all away
And when niggling thoughts would me befall
She'd 'shoo' them off and make them small
Life's lessons from this friend I've learned
To her with confidence I've turned
Encouraged me to know my worth
To fill - with pride, my place on earth
'Be just and fair' my friend would say
She made me what I am today
Each faltering step not in my grasp
Her ever willing hand I'd clasp
Such loyalty each day I'd ride
I simply took it in my stride
Oh selfish me - I raved and ranted
I took this special friend for granted
She smoothed my path, took on my care
I thought she always would be there
But time has passed - hope she can see
How much she really meant to me
For this dear friend could be no other
Than the one I'm proud to call - *my mother.*

Barbara Davies

TIME WAS

Time was when we were young
It's passing without real meaning
And scarcely realised slipped away
In days, months, years beyond redeeming

Time was when with reluctant feet
We resented school bell chimes
But later in a reminiscent mood
Mused fondly on those far off times

Time was when with shining eyes
Saw a future all bright and clear
Ambition beckoned to spur us on
To face life's troubles without fear

Time was when friends abounded
Familiar and thus easy to define
Once real they pass unrecognised
Into the dark abyss of passing time

Time was when the world was dark
Compelling many to weep and mourn
But light returned and when it came
Gave welcome thanks to greet the dawn

But time that was alas is now
Life's full circle almost complete
With most ambitions largely spent
Only a fickle memory remains replete

M F Base

JEANETTE

You've lived in Alnwick and Craster
And now you're at Peep O Sea
Everyone who's ever known you
I'm sure they would agree
You're a very special person
With a heart of gold
You bring such great happiness
Into the lives of young and old
You have so much vitality
Always on the go
Nothing seems a trouble
As such kindness you always show
Each and every one of us
Wherever we chance to meet
Be it at your own home
Or an encounter in the street
Your nice smile is so warming
It could melt a heart of stone
With your great love of others
You'll never be alone
You've such a lovely family
Of which you can be proud
Your personality sparkles
You stand out in a crowd
It's not because we're cousins
I give credit where it's due
Jeanette believe me when I say
I'm truly proud of you

Doreen Quince

MOTHERS ARE SPECIAL

Mothers come only in ones
such special love to share.
A ray of sunshine each new day
which nothing can compare.

Being there throughout the year
to love and understand.
That unique touch warming the heart
a gentle helping hand.

Through all ups and downs of life
a shoulder for to lean.
A list'ning ear and words to calm
those storms such kindness seen.

Great fear and pain then overcome
such love to ever show.
Support, comfort always found
all blessings to bestow.

So thank you Mum for your care
for all the joys you bring.
Much happiness you radiate
simply for everything.

Margaret Jackson

MOTHER'S DAY

Many may feel surrounded with grief
Many may watch for the postman to open the gate
Inspiration only make belief
Someone spare a thought for the lonely who
Would like a posy of flowers to say
Thinking of you on Mother's Day
Knowing someone perhaps all alone
Bunch of daffodils
Wouldn't go wrong
Little bunch in child's tiny hand
Cheery word
Smile of a child
Won't cost much
'Twill last for many a day
The cheer of a child
Bringing sunshine to a mother
Lonely forgotten on Mother's Day
Show kindness to the aged and lonely
Take time to read and pray
The seed you sow will grow you known
We too may be old and lonely some day.

Frances Gibson

JUST A FEW YEARS

I've made friends
In my lifetime
That I say are unique
Not the average person
We have passed on the street
A dear friend that I was
So lucky to share
Just a few years
Precious hours
Here and there
She was gentle and sweet
So intelligent, smart
And the memories of her
Are here in my heart
She touched my life briefly
For those few short years
A special lady, my friend
Who I loved most dear

Jeanette Gaffney

To Louie

A family member from three generations back
We met again through our love of music
We saw each other through so much
She dressed me for my wedding.

We saw each other through the 84/85
The what!
The 84/85 Mine Workers Strike
When all in this valley of the Dearne
Pulled together, so valiantly.

Louie visited me each day
Saw me through hard times
Times when my dear in-laws were dying
When I couldn't buy new clothes.

Louie clothed me from the Scouts 'nearly new'
I will always value her help and support
Support which now includes her two little
Girls (now full grown)
Her mother and her sisters

God bless them all

Janet Cavill

THE HURT I FEEL

When you're lying there beside me, so snuggled up and warm,
I think of what it could have been, how this could have been the norm,
For when I met your brother, we seemed to get on great,
But for long it did not last, maybe we're lucky fate,
For these spirits came and got him, took him away from me,
The hurt in which has broke my heart, pain no one else could see,
But when I touch you, and I look down at your face,
I sometime feel that you're there, to stand in at his place,
And when I kiss you, your face is oh so close,
Feeling the warmth of his breath, is a feeling I'll miss most,
But now that he's gone, we'll get through it together,
Cause we've got that special bond, so we'll last forever.

Julie Titchener

FIFTY YEARS BETWEEN
(Written after watching my dear partner, on his fiftieth birthday holding my first grandchild - born on that day.)

I watched with love as you reached out
And touched that small frail child,
That was of me.
How tenderly you spoke, as lovingly you held
Those limbs, which only hours before
Had known the turmoil of awakening
Into this world of hate and treachery.
My eyes were filled with tears as I observed
You gently stroke that minute scrap
Of flesh and blood - child of my child.
Did you transmit, through gentle hands,
The strength to face this complex world?
Did you bestow on him your powers
To make this world a better place to be?
And did your talents flow into those infant hands
And give him creativity?
My dearest wish is that this child,
Who chose to share with you his day of birth,
Should also share the precious gifts that God has given you.

June M Wilson

A 'MISSING' LIFE

I was just a little girl,
For ten whole years,
A happy life for all that time,
But sadness came in the next nine.

My mum - she left my dad -
Another house - no dad there,
It never did seem right
From morning until night.

I was fed, I was clothed,
I went to school,
But I never did know,
Why it had to be so.

At last grown up, I went to work,
But along came a war -
Another change for many more years,
Rations, bombs and many fears.

At last the sun came through,
When I met you -
Happy and contented -
My life was cemented!

Cindy White

FOR MY CHILDREN

I passed a woman on the street
her stockings hung about her feet
she was unscrubbed, her hair not combed
had she no place, had she no home?
And I thought as I went by
she could be I, she could be I.

What made her be this sorry state,
was it written, was it her fate
that she should lose all dignity
and miss out in life's lottery.
And I knew as I passed by
It could have been I, it could have been I.

You cannot tell how life turns out
how it will turn and turn about.
But I know that I am blessed
with your dear hearts who mind me, least
I should fall and lose my way.
With pride I thank you deep and true
For all your care that lets me say
it won't be I, it won't be I.

Gill Sharma

To My Brother, George

You, were my childhood friend
I didn't need another
We played, we cycled, fished and rode
You were my loving brother
But one day that all had to change
You had to go to war
You left our home to join the lads
That had become the law
All boys and men were called upon
To go and save their country
You loved the life right from the start
And you felt it was your duty
To help bring back the longed-for peace
The hope of everyone
That soon the wrteched war would cease
And all you boys come home
But that just wasn't meant to be
You did your best, you gave your all
And instead of coming back to me
You were left behind, your name now on a wall
A wall of remembrance away abroad
Which I will never see
But I still remember the brother I adored
Who was a friend to me

J E Bishop

OUR LIVES HAVE BEEN CHANGED

I write this verse
So you may know
That I love you.

I know things are difficult
Now things have changed.
Not knowing what the day
Will bring.

It is hard for me too,
When things do not go to plan.
When illness strikes
And I need to rest.

I know you care
And love me in your own way.
I pray my illness will not
Get in the way.

That you will understand,
That this is how it is.
Our lives have been changed.

Despite my illness,
I can still do things.
Please do not shut me out.

I will wait for you
As long as it takes,
Because I love you.

Julie Smith

MY FAMILY

This poem of my family could be rather long,
because there are ten of us for me to dwell upon.
First of all there is my dad, head of the family,
he's worked so hard all of his life which sets the standard for me.

Next there is Mum who's always there with love, laughter and tears
who's always taught us right from wrong sharing our joys and fears.

My eldest brother Christopher, I just call him Chris,
is Staff Sergeant in the RE and he's the one I miss
because he is so far away and has to work so much
I see him maybe once a year, we write to keep in touch.

Tony too is a married man, has children 1 - 2 - 3
his eldest girl is of my age, but I am her auntie.

Then comes bearded brother John, cheerful, hardworking chappie,
because he always laughs a lot his friends nicknamed him 'Happy'.

My sister Marie helps daughter Michelle and me with our
                                          homework a lot
she makes us try to do it when we think we cannot.

Stephen is the youngest man, who just kept teasing me,
but now he has two children and is more brotherly.

Caroline next, she lives on a farm and works from morning till night,
has two little children called Bobbie and Ross and is always
                                          happy and bright.

Sonia as the seventh child is now aged twenty-three
and even though she too works hard, she still finds time for me.

The youngest one - Alicia - am I, soon twelve to be . . .
I'm trying hard to follow on in the good footsteps of my family.

Alicia Dowrick

CHILDHOOD REINS

When we are young we depend upon Mum
She cooks our meals, she buys our clothes,
She nurtures our young lives.

As we grow up we eagerly strive for freedom
We no longer need our childhood reins.
Our parents may find it hard to let go
But that's the only way to help us grow
into mature, responsible adults.

We become parents ourselves
and the process begins all over again.

Cathy Mearman

THE TEARDROP

It said a hundred things to us . . .
'Now don't go making too much fuss
I love you all so very much
I'll miss your mother's gentle touch
I want to stay but don't know how
I really must be going now
I know you love and care for me
Don't worry Ducks, I am pain free
My fight has gone, we have to part
I'm sad to go, it breaks my heart
I'm grateful that you've all been near
I've seen the Lord, and have no fear
Be there for each other, look after your mum
Give a big kiss to my great grandson
Thank family and friends for showing they care'
When I needed help, I knew they were there
Enjoy the memories of the good times we've had
Get on with your lives and don't be too sad'
Dad reassured us at the end,
With the only sign that he could send . . .
A teardrop.

Ena Lynne Chambers

LITTLE CHILDREN

Sweet as a rose, sharp as a thorn!
Little devils at times, angels with horns
Bringing joy, and elation, to complete devastation
They must be God's finest little creations

Reborn I'm sure they are Bonnie and Clyde
One following the other, they play side by side
Taking, breaking, denying their actions!
Can't help falling they are fatal attractions

Overflowing with laughter, and bubbly things
The warmth of feeling their sunshine brings
Endless questions of when, where and why
Precious moments that no money can buy

Seems like yesterday they wanted ice-cream and cake
Destroying the kitchen with biscuits they'd make
Now they are grown, in life, making their way
'Little children', how I wish you were still here today.

Karl Jakobsen

Dead To The World

The dream's not finished
and the phone keeps ringing
the radio's on, I can hear people singing,
are you ready for percolated coffee she's bringing?
Not her only son
just the one who lives at home.

P M Richards

FAMILY TIES

Family ties can be very demanding
For young children are most commanding
Babies need looking after the most
Where toddlers are needing a host

Then from five to teenage years
There will be lots of laughter
Along with all of the tears
For both parents and children too
And forcing children into doing something
They do not wish to do

Even through your adulthood years
This does not always stop here
Whether you're male or female
Some people don't like to fail

Coleen Bradshaw

MY SPECIAL MUM

This poem is written for you mum,
To let you know you're my number one!
You help me to cope when things get tough,
You keep me going when I've had enough!

Your thoughtfulness is always clear,
And that loving nature so very dear.
I love you Mum, so very much,
You always have that special touch!

I hope you know I appreciate all
You do for me, big or small.
I will always help you, if I can,
Like you've helped me, and 'my little man'!

So just you remember, you'll always be
Not just my mum, but a best friend to me.
Without you here, however would I cope,
You've shown me the way, and given me hope!

Thanks - my special Mum!

Patricia Daly

FAMILY

You was not wanted and not fed,
It broke our hearts to see you there,
Not loved, not cared for by anyone,
Only me and your grandfather,
So we sat and talked about the love we shared for you,
And we believed God had answered our prayers,
As me and your grandfather could not have a little boy like you,
So we stepped in and instead of being afraid,
You flourished like life itself,
Your smile so big so much love you give,
Your love so rare but you show you care,
Even though we found you have difficulties,
Such as ADHD and other things,
We will always be there for our little boy,
As love will see us through,
The hard and the good times.

Sandra Pickering

MOTHER

As a mother myself I'm learning fast
What it means to give all the time,
Of patience, time, understanding and love.
Minutes I would like to be mine.

And as I look back on my years as a child,
Growing up in a home filled with love.
I realise how much you gave dear Mum,
More than I understood.

I cannot repay all the love that you gave,
And I know you wouldn't expect
Any thanks, or gifts or garlands.
But you're great Mum - one of the best!

Anne Sharples

YOUR MOTHER

She is the one to whom you turn when no one else is there.
She is the one you always know will understand and care.
She is the one to listen when you really need to talk.
She is the one beside you when you need to take a walk.
She is the one to guide you and the one to show the way.
She is the only one you know will be there night and day.
She is the one to burden with your troubles and your pain.
She is the one who gave you life and gave to you your name.
She is the only one you've got, there'll never be another.
No bond you have can be more strong than this one with your mother.

S Brown

MY SPECIAL SISTER

I had a special sister,
Darling Kate was her name
And though at times she was so ill,
She never laid the blame.

Her smile was like the sunshine,
That brightened up dull days
And whenever I was feeling down,
She cheered me up always.

She had such kind and caring ways,
And this I truly mean.
Even though her work was hard,
She proved that she was keen.

She cared so for her family,
Who loved her very dear.
Day by day and night by night
Year after year.

Kate is so very greatly missed,
By all who loved her so.
But with God's love and faithfulness,
We'll meet again I know.

Teresa Street

FAMILIES

Happy families,
Sad families,
Some families don't care,
Without a family your life is quite bare.
Non-loving families,
Loving families,
Whichever you are,
You're as special as the brightest star.

Jamielee Mackness (10)

You Were Always There

All through my life,
You were always there,
In all my thoughts,
You were always there,
Now I'm alone,
What can I do,
All my life, I had you.

Now part of my heart is empty,
And all I can do is cry.
I miss you so much,
Is that why I hurt,
Would someone tell me why.

Now all of my days are longer,
And I still hear your voice in my head,
Though I am bereaved,
I still can't believe,
I'll come to terms, somebody said.

But all through my life,
You were always there,
In all my thoughts,
You were always there,
Now I'm alone,
What can I do,
All my life, Mum, I had you.

P A Kelly

THANK YOU

Thank you Mum and Dad for everything
Having taught me to be a good individual
And how to love and trust and be happy
Not restricting me, just letting me grow
Kisses, hugs and love are always a plenty
You have been there for me through good and bad
Open to hear what I have to say. Please remember
Us, as a family, is still very important to me.

Lindsey Brown

MY SMILEY STAFFIE

The troubles I told you, you kept to yourself
Never judging, just giving ever more of yourself
You gave me your time without any strings
My loyal and faithful friend to the end.

In my darkest moments, you gave me such peace
Only you understood and could make them cease
Looking deep in your eyes so gentle and brown
Hands stroking your coat, real contentment I found

A decision had to be made one fateful day
Your old body had grown too tired and worn out to stay
You needed your peace and begged to go
It was for the best, but how it hurt me so

Part of me died on that sad day too
My days were left empty so void of you
The pad of your paws I still hear on the floor
The snuffling of your nose as you open the door

You dived into shopping bags looking for a treat
And followed me at mealtimes waiting for your meat
Your gentleness and patience with the kittens shown
As they played in your bed and fell asleep on your bone

Memories are forever in my broken heart
Especially the day you ate up all the tart
It was meant for our callers as you well knew
Who visited us regularly at half past two

Your smiley staffie face I miss each and every day
Especially when you would wake me in your own funny way
The house is so silent and oh so still
Without my friend and companion Bill

Diane Newby

HELEN

To see you sitting there
So calm and serene
Taking pride in everything
Or so it always seems

Knowing you're my daughter
With a child of your own
Knowing how you have given him
Such a loving home

To watch you play with David
Overwhelms me with joy
Seeing him so healthy, sunny
What a lovely boy

Another baby on the way
To fill your life with joy and fun
Knowing now your life's work
Will never ever be done

Your deep and understanding ways
Your forethought and your caring
Your kindliness and wisdom
Which you are always sharing

Loving you the way I do
Not that it's oft times said
May seem sentimental
When this poem's read

Love Mum

Iris Williams

GIFT OF LOVE

For the gift of love
You gave to me
J'taime

For the home so warm
You gave to me
J'taime

For the happiness of children
You gave to me
J'taime

For all the beautiful memories
You gave to me
J'taime

In memory of all things
You left me
J'taime

Hazel V Wood

MY PARENTAGE

Nature, now will run its course,
Thanks to the act, of sexual intercourse.
'His' action became, the father, who is mine,
Took less than a minute, of his time.
The woman, to be, a mother for me,
Became the receptacle, to carry me.
Am I to live, or must I die,
They decide, as my cells multiply.
Aghast, I will be, of being hurt,
Should my development, they abort.
While I depend on my mother's feed,
Smoke, drinks, drugs, I have no need,
Nourishment is what my body will need.
Until my confinement I did succeed,
My future, will be planned for me,
Nine months from that day of their sexuality.

Brian Marshall

GOODNIGHT SWEETHEART

A goodnight kiss blown from afar
Is nestled in a twinkling star
It watches you while I'm away
And keeps you safe another day
Bless your sleep with dreams so sweet
And lay the world before your feet
This pendant orb's been set in motion
So sail your ship upon the ocean
The ocean's wide, the ocean's deep
So let its waves rock you to sleep
To watch and wish and wait and dream
Of candy kisses on clouds of cream

Vanessa Rivington

MY TREASURE

One night, while feeling sad at heart,
How much I wanted to make a fresh start.
Not knowing just, when or where,
I would meet someone to show me care.

Then, all at once, out of the blue,
Happy was I, when I first met you.
While alone, watching TV I sat,
My phone then rang, together we did chat.

Arrangements we made for a meeting,
How happy the words, of our first greeting.
From that very day, there was no looking back,
Happiness now, no longer to lack.

We are both 'Nutty', this is so true,
How much my darling, do I love you.
Whatever comes, no matter the weather,
Happy now, are our lives we share together.

June F Allum

LILITH PASSING BY

Her face lit up as though
For a kiss
But we passed like strangers
That night in the street
My Lilith that was
Before Eve,

Why did we meet before
Why did we love before
Why meet again now?
Oh joy of an old love
Waking!

But gone again now
Gone down the street
My Lilith that was
Before Eve.

Michael Rowson

GOLDEN WEDDING MEMORIES

Our love is like a tiny bud that blossomed into flower,
Well tended by the hand of God it perfumed every hour.
It all began so suddenly, became a deep desire,
A tiny spark within our hearts burst forth in flaming fire.

And now this love forever true is like a golden chain,
A memory sweet each tiny link, together we remain.
Fifty years have sped away since we made our wedding vow
We travelled through the stormy times and weathered them till now.

The children of our union brought us happiness at birth,
Our love for them we hope they'll spread to others here on earth.
Our love brings out my thankful praise for your loyalty and care,
And the years that now remain, by God's good grace we'll share.

Beryl R Daintree

MIDNIGHT MOMENT

Silently I stand and watch
As the midnight hour slowly passes.
Calm, serene and innocent,
Such beauty in your sleeping face my son.
Gentle breathing and the occasional sigh
Fills the quiet room.

What sweet thoughts pass through your mind?
What games do you play whilst you dream?

Soon you sense my being.
A sleepy eye opens and meets mine in intimate embrace
Followed by a smile of such warmth
That you and I become one for a fleeting moment.
Hands touch, two souls entwine and
Sleep calls you back into that world beyond my reach.

Glenn Lewis

My Mother's Wardrobe

As a seven year old
My mother's wardrobe
Was forbidden to me
So naturally I spied while she was out

Ignoring the mundane, falling on two dresses
That caught my eye.
Evening dresses from the thirties
When she had time for such frivolity

Pink chiffon swathed, I pranced
In front of the mirror
Bugle beads twinkling brightly
A fur complete with fox's head
Beady eyes of glass stared
At me accusingly.

And then the biggest prize of all
The cosmetics and jewellery
Face powdered, lips of ruby-red
I decked myself with beads and bracelets
Admiring my reflection in the mirror

Many years later I can still remember
The scent of Evening in Paris and
Coty face powder.
And I think of my mother.

Adrianne Jones

EMPTY PROMISES

As darkness falls
I think of you
I dream you'd hold me
Like you used to

Remembering the times
The love that we shared
The security in knowing
How much you cared

Where has it gone
Where is it now
I thought it'd come back
But it's gone somehow
Empty words and silent dreams
Promises . . . were they empty promises?

Just one perfect moment
Is all you allow
I want to talk
But I just don't know how

So much to say
So little time
All I want is you
To be mine

Somehow I don't think
I will see you again
We've drifted apart through the years
But then you are still you
And I am still me
So where are these promises
Can you show me what you mean?

Lisa Bennett

BONBON

Bonbon was a little cat
Who liked to lie down on the mat
And thought that it was rather dire
If someone moved her from the fire
She had her place upon the stair
Move her only if you dare
Out she'd go and catch a mouse
And try to bring it in the house
Then when it was time for a feed
She'd let you know she was in need
Oh dearie me if she was ill
The fuss and bother to give her a pill
Bonbon her name, it was just right
As she was such a Sussigkeit

Moira H Thorburn

IN MEMORY OF MELVINA

The smoky voice,
The happy laugh,
The light step forward.
You gave all -
The fighter.

That tiny frame,
So full of promise,
That bright flame
Burning to the end.
The fighter.

We've shared your life.
We've watched you fight.
We've always loved you.
We'll always remember,
The fighter.

Rose-Marie Bonnevier

PRAYING FOR FAMILIES

As we pray for our families, Lord,
I pray you will consider mine.

There are nephews in Greenwich and Cripplegate,
in Southampton and Milford Haven,
in Fulham and Tooting
and one about to retreat, near Athens.
There are brothers in York and Wales
and commuting between Suffolk and Oxford.
There are sisters in Battersea and Hammersmith
and the ancients are in Kensington.
We have a son in Queensland, Australia
and a daughter in Dogthorpe.
My wife is at home in Colchester,
while I am on the road to a hotel in Bradford

Lord you are all seeing and omnipresent.
As I pray for my family, Lord,
this is just as well.

David W Lankshear

PARENTHOOD

We bring them into this old world
A product of our pleasure
We cherish them as tiny babes
So dependent, at our leisure

We feel so proud each step they take
Each time our praise they win
We take so much for granted and
So soon the time is gone

They tell us much of all the joys
The pleasures of parenthood
But not how lost we're going to feel
When we say goodbye, good luck

It's then we sit and wonder
Were we really good enough
Did we give them all the time
The care, the love we're capable of

Did we teach them how to survive
This ugly cruel world
Yet consider other people
In action, thought and word

Did we teach them how to love
And be loved in return
And not to take for granted
All the pleasures of this world

The only thing we can say is
I'm here if you need me
And hope they grow in confidence
Rich, full content lives to lead

Christine Lockton

TO GOOD OLD TOM

Here's to my hubby, who's given to me
The best in life, which wasn't free,
He's been tried and tested, in such a hard world,
And he's come out the best, it now can be told.

Fighting and trying to save his life
When the old, old world was ablaze with strife,
Then battling again for somewhere to live,
The best he could find, his family to give.

When this was achieved, another battle was sought
To find the best work, so food could be bought,
He cycled for miles, every day, not once, but twice
He never failed to live up to his girth and splice.

Then troubled illness, at home, for his wife,
He worked out a plan for children and life,
He saw it all through, the bitter years of strife,
But was successful again, away went all the grief.

So here we all are, a great family tree,
Which would never have been, were it not for he
Who had such an awful, wicked start to life,
So well done! Tom, and it's with love from your wife.

Phyllis Wright

A Special Person

You are such that you cannot see
The courage you show in adversity.
The optimism you daily display
With your problems here to stay.

The shoulder you offer for others to cry on
The deeds that you do that others rely on.
The gracious air you exude as you go
The trouble you take to ensure we don't know.

How difficult it can be for you just to walk straight
The efforts you make not to arrive late.
The struggle you have to do all your chores
Your limitations lessened or completely ignored.

Your smile lights our day with your cheerful news
Of hobbies and interests, of snooker and cues.
Your singing voice a joy to us all
Not a hint or clue of your latest fall.

When you wave 'goodbye, see you soon'
I welcome you back, you're a boon.
Your positive attitudes seem daily to grow
You're an example to us all, a pleasure to know.

Gloria Hargreaves

A MOTHER'S LOVE

The unconditional love of a mother
One can compare to no other
When they said this time it's a boy
My heart was filled with love and joy
And with two daughters and a son
I knew life would not lack fun

I tended your needs with love and devotion
Experiencing every kind of emotion
Your smiles brought happiness beyond measure
Your first words were moments to treasure
And as I watched your achievements with pride
I vowed to always be on your side

Often when the going got tough
We'd take the smooth times with the rough
In a family united our troubles we shared
Showing each other how much we cared
Teenage years were filled with drama
And I was there through every trauma

Now you all have lives of your own
And I am back where I started alone
But still I share your joys and sorrow
Reminding you of that new day tomorrow
When with families of your own to guide
You'll know a parent's love and pride

Now I fear my life draws to a close
As I sit here in my chair and doze
And when it's time for us to part
Keep somewhere special in your heart
For me, your proud and devoted mother
Whose love can be likened to no other.

Pamela Di Nicoli

TRUTH HURTS

The truth hurts,
Doesn't it just!
I really wish, I could,
Tell you.

But - I just can't,
Don't you see!
It hurts me too,
You will see.

One day, understand,
It's better this way,
I have lost friends,
I could lose you.

End of term will come,
Then, 'it'll be all over',
Our friendship will last,
Become stronger.

Only then, I'll tell you,
Why, things are as they are,
Then, I really hope,
You will understand.

Tammara M Wilband

FAMILY TIES
(In memory of a friend)

Pepper died today,
The world is sad and grey
Without my friend

She's just a dog you tell yourself
The chairs are free from hair
The garden grass is pristine green
But nothing can compare
With wagging tail and big brown eyes
To greet you at the door
A loving nose upon your lap
Devotion that is pure.

Satisfied to feel your hand
Resting on her head
To climb the stairs and settle down
Content beside your bed
The tears are never far away
Pepper died today.

Audrey Willis

A MESSAGE TO MY CHILDREN

Often it is difficult
To tell them, how you feel.
Your children know, you love them.
So, on an even keel,
You steer your way through life.

I love you - I appreciate you
Are thoughts, not often said aloud.
You think, they know, what's in your heart,
And that of them you're always proud;
That you are there for them in strife.

But don't you know, how good it feels,
When someone says: I love you.
This message to my children now:
- I love you strong and true!

Helga Dharmpaul

SISTER

You're my sister and my friend
When I'm with you I don't have to pretend
You can be anything you want to be
You accept me for being me
Sometimes we fall out
Usually we never remember what it was about
Friends will come and go
But I'll always know
You will always be there
I want to let you know I care
We weren't brought up to say it out loud
You'd almost think it wasn't allowed
So I wrote it here for you to read one day
Then you'll know it doesn't have to be that way

Amanda Steel

WHO?

No childhood photographs,
To show me what I've been,
All you gave was nothing,
But the crest of a dream,
With no wisdom of a mother,
Tell me who should I be?
In my sight a thousand shadows,
Which one of them is me?

J Hatton

CINDY

My angel has left me
No matter how far
She looks down to guide me
The brightest of stars.

The garden is empty
For what could replace
That soft furry creature
Her style, full of grace.

The robin is fearless
And follows me round
So close I could touch her
She swoops on the ground.

A beautiful creature
A joy to behold
But nothing replaces
My angel now cold.

Pamela Dibden

SIMON

I have not wanted to commit you to the page
It must be some poetic superstition
As if by doing so I somehow lessened you.
How can I describe what you are to me
How I see you, what you mean to me?
I have been reading 'After Apple Picking' by Robert Frost,
And thinking about mortality,
That you might be reading this when I am dead.
Strange thought, because here I am now
And I can't imagine a time
When you are here and I'm not.
This is getting like a letter;
It wasn't meant to be a farewell
Or a testament to be opened after death.
It's about life, our life, our lives, us.
What more can I say? - I love you.

Michael Thorpe

THE LIGHT
(For Farah)

My lovely daughter
Please don't ever change
Don't let the world deprive you
Of your love of life.
Your smile, your laugh,
Those parts of you
That shine out like a beacon
In the dark.
The gift of happiness
You scatter in your wake
Leaves other, sadder hearts
Uplifted still,
And when the dust has settled
From your passing through
The memory of your presence
Long remains.
My lovely daughter
What a light you are.
Shining alone
Amongst a galaxy of stars.

Lynda E Tavakoli

MATCHSTICK LIMITS

See the world through the eyes of a collective child
Big heads full of family mythology:
One thin body, fat head of clan thought undefiled,
Claustrophobic that related community.

Hope to journey further than the perimeter
But the family somersaults to keep you in shape -
A fence, their defensive, emotional barrier
Yet somehow they have you tethered if you escape.

Pulling the post is fraying the rope grown beyond:
Filling out: fat and three dimensional,
Whirling distantly from that suffocating bond.
If tribal twigs snap - that was unintentional.

Hypnotised by glowing freedom of flame
Melting clone to strike out alone - burning the frame!

Suzanne Stratful

EDWIN

he fell on his head
poor Ted
drunk, always drunk
now dead

they carried him
he weighed a ton
followed by his wife, two daughters and a son
pretending for the last time to love him

no more grief
only relief

Alfa

MEMORIES ARE ALL I HAVE LEFT

Somehow I had always thought that you would be near,
And protecting me, I would have nothing to fear.
But then suddenly, without warning, you left me,
I'm feeling as unhappy as person can be.

In my sadness, I remember all the good times,
There's not a day goes by when you're not on my mind.
Think of your smile and the way that you laughed out loud,
Personality made you stand out in a crowd.

I wish that today you could be here by my side,
Some memories have made me laugh 'til I cried.
Not sure I will ever get used to losing you,
Promise to live my life as you'd want me too.

S Mullinger

THANK YOU

Thoughts of the past started to fly.
I felt love before, only to see it die.
And yet again - I try.
Another love, another chance.
You helped me take a risk
On a love that could last.
You say nothing's too good for me.
I only wish that you could see,
By saying those words and so many like,
You're already too good for me.
They can't see what I've found in you.
They never even tried.
Just looking upon the surface
And never what's inside.
So thank you for letting me know you,
Just as well as you know me,
And for letting me again believe in love,
And showing me how amazing it can be.

Gemma Louise Cole

FAMILY TIES . . . ALL LAID TO REST

The truth and tradition of family ties . . .
Is laid to rest, for they have died.
Isolated pockets still reside . . . in isolated hearts.

Once upon a time . . . most everyone . . .
Had family . . . to rely upon.
You may still find one? In an isolated heart.

Now we put restrictions on . . . selfless love . . .
Reserved for self . . . even God above
Must push and shove . . . to get his share.

Husbands live with . . . interchanging wives.
Swap over lives
Contrive . . . to steal a share.

Only someone like You . . . or Him . ..
Give love, full to the brim
Don't prune or trim . . . or make demands.

Yet even then . . . no one speaks aloud . . .
For they walk with anonymous crowd
Too vain . . . or much too proud
To say . . . *I love!*

Brenda Robson-Eifler

SEVENTY-SIX TROMBONES

Happy birthday for the last time Grandad.
Lion courage keeps you laughing, living.
As your mind paints the next picture, I'm glad
To sense the joy your artist's hand can bring.

'Seventy-six. Seventy-six trombones,'
You said. I see these years in your blue eyes.
You worked and worked like the sea shaping stones.
Suffered no fools, always early to rise.

Thanks for introducing me to Arsenal.
We follow not blindly the Club's support.
One of your passions, live life to the full.
You are strong, proud, chased but never once caught.

Stephen Wren

SILENT JUDGEMENT

At about ten forty-five,
Cage covered for the night,
Our guest budgerigar would climb sideways down his ladder
For a minute late supper.

Once, he delayed returning to his height.
From a nearby chair, I looked up to see
Two penetrating eyes steadily fixing me;
A motionless body near a low perch,
Claws grasping the railings;
A black and white wig;
Two ounces of fluff, in the dim light,
Silently weighing me up,
Judging me unhurriedly.

Those unperturbed beady eyes humbled me,
Made me feel ill at ease.
What did he know?
What did he think?
Why didn't he say?

An uncanny experience this!

Then, apparently satisfied, and without pronouncing judgement,
He left the court and mounted his ladder,
Leaving me wondering forever.

Dora Hawkins

A GOLDEN FUTURE

I remember so clearly
  The day you were born,
    So fragile yet tough,
      To your life we were sworn.

With a life not so bright,
  Like a light you shone,
    And your dad with delight,
      Declared, 'This is Shawn'.

Each day we struggle,
  And find pathways new,
    To enjoy all of life,
      Each day is our cue.

You bring so much to my life,
  Whether in pain or in joy,
    The future is golden,
      Please grab, and enjoy.

Tricia

My Guardian Angel

When I try to find the words for you,
My brain gives up with a sigh,
Because there are no words that can explain to the world,
How important you are in my life.

You're always there when I need you,
Your love fills me like sunshine in my head,
A summer's day reminds me so much of you,
Bringing happiness and smiles we've shared.

You are wise and funny and patient,
Everything that I want to be,
I admire you much more than you realise,
Because it's the real you I see.

You're there to chase away ghosts in the night,
And there to catch me when I fall,
Everyone around you adores you, like me,
Because your love encompasses them all.

You've always been my best friend,
Because we're there for each other,
I love you so much for all that you are,
And thank God that I have you as a mother.

With all my heart.

Suzanne Nicholls

SISTER

A sister is someone on who you can depend,
she is not only your companion but your dearest, closest friend.
You only have to call her if you're feeling blue,
she is someone who will always listen, and who you can tell your
problems to.
She will share your laughter and your tears,
a sister's bond grows stronger with the passing of the years.
I would like to say to my sister, a thank you for all the good times,
all the laughter and the fun.
I have so many happy memories, and you're part of every one.
Things seem to get even better with the passing of time,
and of all the sisters in the world, I am so glad that you are mine.
To me my sister's love is special, and it's been like that right
from the very start,
so these are not just empty words I write for they are written
from my heart.
These words are a tribute to my sister, to say thank you for
always being there,
and for all the things you do for me and showing that you care.
I know I don't always say that much, but I do have feelings deep inside,
when people say is that your sister, I say 'yes she is' with pride.

Melinda Evans

MY MOTHER'S BOUQUET

Carnations, crushed, in the lemon-rind light.
Tissues in the Mercado, rustling
Carmine, violet, indigo, red.
Bleeding rainbows, lively as the dead, preserved
In a blanket, in a Mexican market.

I called from Guadalajara;
Old women gossip and complain.
But you filled your glass with joie de vivre,
Citrus drops of aqua libre.
You said you'd had the flowers I sent:
The lights of spring - aubergine bites of aconites,
Scented, chromatic, sulphuric irises,
The butter-fluff sambucas racemosa.

This is the day of the dead.
Castanets. Footsteps in an empty *cathedral.*

I found the packet-seed dreams you buried away
Between the scales of a paper moth;
Lilac candy-tufts, which never could and can take flight.
The perfume of your powder. Clots in my veins.

I call down the stars, shut off the sun
And leave. Dead flowers. Frosts in the night.

Gill Morgan

THE SPECTACLE

I stare, standing, in amazement.
Two entities looking up at me.
From where were they sent?
Unbelievable! Can it really be?

Their language develops in stages -
First, cries of need and frustration,
Then murmurs, words, and reading from pages.
Progressing to loving, friendly conversation.

Beauty and innocence entwined, so meek.
O wondrous entities, so mild.
To see their smiles, to hear them speak.
The wondrous spectacle of the child.

Martin Short

A FRIEND IN NEED

Just when you thought you couldn't cope.
Just when you thought you were alone, unable to carry on.
Just when you thought the world was a bleak place, full of gloom,
                                               shadows and fears.
Just when you felt your confidence ebb, sucked into a swamp
                                               of doubts . . .

A familiar voice breaks into your thoughts.
A familiar smile lights up your day.
A friend who knows you well,
A friend whose familiar presence gives you strength.
A friend indeed.

Julia Pattison

COURTNEY LOU

Peek-a-boo Courtney Lou,
Peek-a-boo my Courtney Lou,
When you smile the sun comes shining through,
I am happy every day, except when you're away,
Peek-a-boo my Courtney Lou, peek-a-boo.

When I'm hurting all the while,
You still can make me smile,
It's a happiness that takes my pain away,
Even though I'm feeling blue, you always pull me through,
Peek-a-boo my Courtney Lou, peek-a-boo.

If the world could see your smiles,
It's a light that shines for miles,
It's so innocent, so pure and so sincere,
You could take their cares away, there'd be peace and love each day,
Peek-a-boo Courtney Lou, peek-a-boo.

Perhaps it's no surprise, I see through Grandad's eyes,
So I'm biased and because you make me smile,
I am happy all the day, except when you're away,
Peek-a-boo, my lovely Courtney Lou.

Ian Hardwick

TO ELVIS

I never could imagine,
That you would not be there
I took your life for granted
I placed you way up there.
Your singing changed the very course
Of music in our lives
We loved you as young women,
We loved you still, as wives.

The shockwaves went right through me
As I first heard the news
Someone had found your body
Now was this just a ruse?

Did you just need a breather
To rest your weary head?
The messages came through then,
That you were really dead.

I didn't cry at first though,
I guess I was too shocked
I sat and wrote a poem
The music world was rocked.

The whole world was in mourning
The king of rock was dead,
Graceland was bombarded
With messages instead.

I still think of you, Elvis
And listen to your voice
You meant something to everyone
For they had little choice.
To love you, or to hate you
But one thing is for certain
They just could not ignore you
Behind the final curtain.

Eileen Burton

MY BEST FRIEND

I walk up my path feeling shattered
Slowly push open the door
To be met with a rapturous greeting
Which nearly knocks me down to the floor.

His tongue frantically licks me
His tail nearly wags off his end
He's my white and black bundle of mischief
He's my loveable dependable friend

He doesn't mind if I'm moody
Just reminds me he's there with deep sighs
Head on paws, always ready
Gazing with love in his eyes

I take down his lead, he's ecstatic
We joyously walk down the lane
Nose to ground, not a scent escapes him
He's in his doggy heaven again

Rabbits anxiously peep from their burrows
As he carefully examines each tree
Then we're running homeward together
Both of us eager for tea

B Bisgrove

TED - MY FRIEND

I don't know how we became friends,
I can't remember when it all began,
It seems as if you've always been there,
I suppose there was a time when I didn't know you,
Many years ago,
When I was young,
And you were young,
We are both older now,
Much older,
I think we've stopped counting the years,
But true friendship survives and outlives the test of time,
Through all of those years I've always known you were my friend,
My true friend,
Reliable,
Caring,
Genuine,
Honest,
And so much more,
We don't live in each other's pockets,
We live our separate lives,
But we both know that the other is there, always.
I never have to ask for your help,
You offer before I can ask,
In times of trouble you are the first one at my door,
A shoulder to cry on,
A supporting hand,
A heart that shares my sadness and gladness,
My burdens and my joys.
Thank you my friend,
My life is greatly enriched by your friendship.

Jim Sargant

CAPTURED ONE'S HEART

(Dedicated to Pepe, my Cairn Terrier,
who only lived, but a short time)

To wait for the day
Will pave the way
With love and care
If only one dare
Shining golden light
Sparkling so bright
Big brown eyes
Which tell no lies
Walking with style
Having a lovely smile
Always able to share
To be totally fair
A trip by car
Was not so far
Bringing one home
Never to be alone
Two as one part
Which captured one's heart

Anthony Higgins

MUM'S LITTLE GARDEN

When my mother was alive
A little garden she did strive
Alas! The vandals came and trod
Right upon the very sod.

Now the vandals have gone away
A little garden has come to stay
My wish for Mum, was her to see
The little garden and her tree.

Sad to say, the wish for me
Was never really meant to be.

Joyce Coultas

APRON STRINGS

Apron strings, apron strings,
Stronger than hawsers of steel;
Yet light as the breath of a kiss,
Built upon emotional blackmail.

Selfish parent, selfish parent,
Willing to sacrifice, sacrifice
Your child, on the altar of self.
Your claim, a service pledge.

Lonely parent, lonely parent,
Demand and expect obedience
A life of catering to your needs
From the 'willing' helpful child.

Scared parent, scared parent,
Willing to forgo the promise
Of grandchildren, for the sure
Guaranteed 'love' of your child.

Naive child, naive adult,
Brought up to be a slave,
Conditioned and trained,
To love and serve others.

Busy child, extra busy adult,
You have to earn a living,
Yet you also have to care;
Now emotionally scarred.

Tired child, burned-out adult,
Now your parent has gone,
Also your life, looks and hopes
Yours is now a barren legacy.

Jean Wearn Wallace

WHY MUM?

Why do I feel
  that I'm to blame?
Why do I feel
  this sickening shame?

When all I needed was a hug.

Why did you shut
  that open door?
Why? Don't you
  love me anymore!

Mum . . . all I wanted was a hug.

Where was your affection
  where I needed to cry?
Why didn't you want me?
  Please tell me why.

Mum . . . all I needed was a hug.

Why were your
  words so insincere
'I love you'
  was all I needed to hear.

And the one thing I wanted was a hug!

Marcus Tyler

SECRET LOVE

To see you from a distance
And I cannot reach and touch
It hurts my heart so sadly
Because I love you oh so much

We have to keep this secret
Between you and me alone
If not for this reason
I'd write or telephone

I love your looks and love your smile
I long to hold you for a while
But this I know cannot be
Although you say that you love me

We steal a little cuddle
And we steal a little kiss
And if you turn away from me
These times I'd really miss

Although you say you love me
I fear we will drift apart
And if this ever happens
You will really break my heart

C C Lee

ANDY BOO

The further away I get from you, the harder it gets for everyone else,
The happier I was with you, the harder it gets when I'm alone.
Further away, it fades your childhood,
Further away you're dazed and misunderstood.
I love you dearly, and I'm praying you're happy.

Since we were kids, I have learnt from you, how to succeed.
You gave me strength, (even when weak) so that I could accomplish
My needs in this world of bionic minds.
You are my mind, heart and soul and now that you've gone,
I am disorientated, but hoping that you are still watching over me,
Making sure that I don't slip.

I hope that you are now resting, with your over-worked mind, so that
Peace can wrap you up in the same cotton wool you covered me in.
I will always cherish your thoughts and motion
That you so honestly gave me.
I hope one day we will meet again in that faraway land where
Again . . . again togetherness, under lock and key.

Helen Gordon

WITH LOVE FOR MUM

Your love has kept us strong through the years
With soothing words you banished our tears
Your kindness is warm like summer sun
When we are lost
It's to you we run
A rainbow has beauty that brightens the sky
But none to compare to the love in your eyes
And a volume of words could never express
How much we love you
For you are the best
In this world there can never be another
We love you dearly our special
Mother

Jacquie Williams

KAREN

You were snatched away far too early
Your time should not have come
How much of life you would have enjoyed
Made a grandmother of your mum
She still visits you nearly all the time
Fresh flowers put in place
When instead she would give her own life
For one glimpse of your smiling face
You were her one and only child
Her ultimate bundle of joy
Having almost eighteen wonderful years
Which a knock at the door can destroy
Such a bright young lady you became
Full of spirit and a loving heart
With prospects flooding at your feet
Which society you would become apart
We cherish your memory, the laughs we had
Me and your mum miss you very much
One day we will all be reunited
When God has chosen us with his touch.

Caryne Crane

MY FATHER'S APPLES

Each new journey,
Each September beginning,
My father sends me
A farewell of apples.

All autumn term
They lingered in cupboards,
Sating the dark
With smell of moss and old vinegar.
Other girls gorged
On loot slick-wrapped
In foils and frostings.
Small, specked, fruit of his eye,
I hid their bruising
In shame or tenderness or pride.

On trains, in desks,
Crammed or tucked
Clumsily in briefcase, drawer,
Their soft tang
Is the flavour of parting.
All through absence
I carry my tokens of Eden -
Dappled by sun and sentiment,
A little misted
By the mind's eye.

Each new journey,
Every September beginning,
Now and for always
This fanfare of apples.

Laura Wilkins

MEMORIES

How many times I long for
the days before I knew,
that life was not as simple
as I'd believed before.
The leaves were dancing merrily
that distant winter morn.
The day that I discovered
my world was not my own.
The family I'd always loved,
who'd always been so dear,
belonged to other children.
I couldn't bear to hear
those awful words, 'you're fostered'.
No child should have to know
their parents did not want them
thrown out, discarded, *why?*
My parents weren't my parents,
my sister wasn't mine.
Which words would keep me going?
We chose a special child.

J Gilbert

A COMFORTABLE MARRIAGE?

I fall into your waves,
the coldness rushes me,
sharp rocks crush me, brush me aside.
I try to breathe, it makes me cry.
You drag me down and I don't know why.
I try to make contact, reach for air,
I know you're deep down but where?
The darkness scares me and I look for the light,
don't punish me because I care, want what's right.
I'll take anything even the gulls that screech,
just show me that hope's not out of reach.
You're typhoons, gusts and a breeze,
eddies, whirlpools and calm seas.
One day will come and you'll smash me aside,
for everyone there's always one wave that they can't ride.
Will I drown with you or will I swim and leave you far behind?
I'll only know when that wave hits my mind.

R M Membury

GRANDAD

Grandad you were so special to me
I remember you well you see
You were Grandad to children in the street
Whatever nationality we chanced to meet
But alas Mum told me about a different time
When you were a rebel and out of line.

Many a time you'd gamble money away
No food on the table what can I say?
A trip to the pub you also enjoyed
This meant no shoes, no clothes and no toys
Grandma would work scrubbing the floors
So that the basics they could afford.

When you grew older you were a gentle man
Our holidays with you and Grandma were planned
You worked very hard, you still had a flutter
There was more on the table than bread and butter
I'd sit on the coal box beside the fire
Enjoying each moment until I'd perspire.

Your garden you tendered with much loving care
It seemed that anything planted would grow there
You earned a prize for flowers you grew
Grandad I was so very proud then of you
School holidays were for me so much fun
To be with you all day to skip and to run.

Grandad you were a rebel it's true
You enriched my life because you were you
I bear you no grudge for stepping out of line
For to me you were so very kind
If only you were here today this I would do
I'd run with arms open and place them round you.

Rosemary Lee

GRANNY GROWING OLD

The groaning bone,
Insistent whine,
She won't let it be shown:
There is no consciousness of time,
She stumbles on and hides her pain.

A walking stick she dare not wield
For time will follow through
And show her years to all the world,
Confirm her fears: she is not new.

She thinks as one who nurtures youth
But where she dwells in flesh and bone:
Not realised as tired and worn,
Her mind is young - but old, so old her home.

She's ancient as antiquity
And now years passed, she bends her knee:
The old one welcomes age at last,
Receives at once great dignity,
'I'm old' she says and smiles at me.

Brenda Dove

REFLECTIONS

Sitting in this garden warm,
Caressed by sun's sleepy waves,
My thoughts drift away, through the corridors of time,
A time of innocence and endless days,
Playing cricket in the street, kiss chase,
Cowboys and Indians, fighting pirates bold,
Standing proudly on mounds of gold,
Fantasy to be blown away by a voice calling, 'Time for tea.'
There will be bread and jam, and cakes if we are lucky!
Father, cycling home, besieged by children four,
'Can we have a penny?' 'A farthing each, no more.'
Excitedly cross the road, to the shop, mind that car!
To claim in each grubby hand, a small toffee bar.
Short trousers turn to long, a time to be strong,
Childish dreams abandoned, real world beckons on.
Soon, teenage excitement dashed, war's ugly head rears,
Devastating scenes, bombing plane's vile drone,
Heads down in shelters deep, no time to weep, hide your fears,
Moving on to happier days, first true love, carries me away.
Sweet kisses, family bond, wife and children take me on.
Some heartaches tinged with sorrow,
For some, there is no tomorrow.
Life must go on, as go on it does, children fly the nest,
To join the rest, on the road of time.
My thoughts return from journeys far and things that I have seen
To blink at the sun,
To give thanks for what I have,
Not what might have been,
With my love by my side, no more childish games,
But, there might be 'jam for tea'!

K L Pusey

GERANIUMS

Sun on:
leaf-dappled pavement
elm tree avenues
city lovers relaxed free
crumbling painted houses faded appealing
red flowers in pots tipsy with glee
people under parasols at white coffee tables
you and me

Carole Luke

MY BEST FRIEND

Mum, you are my best friend
You mean the world to me,
Maybe I don't often tell you
But words don't come too easily.

You are always there for me
A shoulder on which to cry,
If I'm down and very miserable
You can always get me by.

When I'm sad or very happy
Of one thing I can be sure,
I can always come to you Mum
Through your ever open door.

Where would I be without you?
I really cannot think.
More times than I remember
Me, you brought back from the brink.

Bless you Mum with all my heart
For all the times you care,
Through tears of grief and sorrow
Of heartache and despair.

Through anger and frustration
And love and kindness too,
I couldn't love you more Mum
Than I already do.

My grateful thanks for years gone by
And for all the years to come,
Forever I send you all my love
For being a very special Mum.

Maureen Gard

MOTHER'S DAY

A mother's love I've sent to heaven
To where your heart is there
Through the clouds and past the stars
Way, way past Jupiter and Mars

Just like a jewel in heaven's key
Where you send your love back home to me
And every time a snowflake falls
You come and visit me

Denis Manley

THANKS PHILIP

I oft recall the hours we've spent
Together, quaffing ale
In pubs by Leith and far off Clent
Where we our spirits would regale
And how those hours so quickly went

The many delightful pubs we found
In Shires of Worcester and of Staffs
In which pint after pint we've downed
Tales told and retold brought us laughs
The last one by the next one crowned

In The Navigation and The Vine
The Boot by Lapworth's waterway
We always found the beer fine
To draw us back another day
Just for a drink, perhaps to dine

There found relief from noonday sun
And in the cool of eve
The pattern of each day would run
So happy the many hours that we've
Shared until each day was done

All those places I hold dear
Hope for those hours to come again
But years roll on, that make me fear
That such a hope may be in vain
Yet in spite of that I'll try to make that trip again
Next year

H H Steventon

FAMILY LOVE

When I first looked upon your face;
Small and folded as a rosebud
In its first opening on the world,
My heart was full of wonder, joy and love,
Of thanks for my first lovely little girl.

I gave you life and ever cared for you;
Loving each moment as you came to grow
Into your childhood, then your womanhood,
Remembering all the gifts we shared, the journeys made
The meetings and the partings, when you went away.

Following you, a brother and two sisters came
To make our family life full and complete.
Now I give thanks that you are all good friends,
That you still come together, share each other's company,
Knowing my love towards you is still strong and true.

Mary Johnson-Riley

My Only Love

It was really love at first sight
Into my life he brought light,
We met cycling when cars were very few,
Our love for each other slowly grew.

We married each other in 1954
Our two daughters we did adore,
It was a marriage of give and take,
So a wonderful marriage we did make.

The marriage lasted forty-four years,
We had laughter, love and tears.
Three years ago sadly he died,
Through happy memories I have survived.

Pamela Earl

THANKS MUM

For helping me when I am low,
And I don't know which way to go.
Thanks Mum.

For soothing my tired and confused soul,
And helping me to stay in control
Thanks Mum.

For times when I do my best
And yet I am put to the test,
You listen, advise and counsel me,
You hear, you share, and you guide me,
Thanks Mum.

For being my friend, sharing ups and downs,
For always being there whether I smile or frown,
For sharing excitement and easing the pain,
That lingers in my heart and seems to remain . . . Thanks Mum.

For helping me to see things through,
For supporting and . . . just for . . .
Being you.

Thanks Mum.

Yvonne M Wright

BYGONE DAYS

The jasmine covered wall hears my call
Its compelling beauty laid at my feet
So to speak.
Equally, the fresh spring country lanes and byroads
Entices me onwards to this land of dreams.
To pause again by shimmering sunlit streams,
My destination
A simple country cottage, white washed walls
And dark old beams, a haven of tranquillity,
A grandmother in a rocking chair
Old and frail, but simply there
Remembering the tread upon the stair
The blue-eyed gentle lover of yesteryear,
Tiny voices remembered, the kettle on the hob
Rice pudding cooking on the stove.
So long ago,
The cottage no longer there
Just a monstrous modern building to compare
Never the same but the vibes are there
Will be there forever
As long as I can return there.

Joan Hands

MY SPECIAL FRIEND

My friend, my very dear friend,
who, as spring turned into summer
and dark clouds rolled away
with the sun brought warmth,
laughter, joy and happiness
and moments to treasure.
And whatever autumn, winter
or future seasons bring for you
or me, you will always have
a special place in my heart
and I hope you will always be
my friend, my very special friend

God bless.

Diana Daley

THE WORLD'S BEST

My mother is my dream come true
She's never ever disrespectful to you
She'll make you laugh when you should cry
She'll comfort you when someone dies

She is a beautiful dancing queen
And no one else can come between
The way we laugh or how we play
It just wouldn't happen not any day

I love my mum more than anything
And I just thought she should know
Because nothing makes me happier than
To see her stunning glow
I love my mum regardless
When times are good or bad

I love you Mum truly
From the daughter you're glad you had!

Charlene Keyes

FRIENDS

There is not much I remember of my childhood days,
But my work brought unique friendships in many different ways.
You see when you are not certain what you might face,
There is really only one answer, meet each hour with grace.
Soon you will realise that there are many around
Who will go out of their way to help keep you safe and sound.

Betty Green

LAST GOODBYE

Goodbye my love it's time to go,
The pain is now starting to show,
The suffering that you have had to endure,
Sleep now my love and worry no more,
A last lingering kiss and words of love,
Your journey will soon start to heaven above,
I know you will have no more pain,
But how will I ever smile again?
You've always been a part of me,
It's going to be hard to set you free,
I know it really is for the best,
It's time for you to go for a long rest,
Close your eyes and go to sleep,
Memories of you I'll always keep,
Together for always we were going to be,
But I know you will be waiting for me,
So though it breaks my heart so,
Goodbye my love, it's time to go.

Sandy

THE KESTREL

He named the ketch, *The Kestrel*. Like her namesake
she hovered, her bow facing the horizon, ready to take
on the racing waves. Two sturdy masts, fore and aft,
completed the perfect balanced lines of the trim craft.
All preparations complete, he was ready now to start:
anticipation and excitement quickening his heart.
The man and boat, in unison and in perfect harmony
began to glide across the bay towards the open sea.
With her scarlet sails filled taut in the offshore wind
The Kestrel gathered speed. A dawn mist had thinned
as she reached deep waters and with a clear sky above
his hand caressed the tiller - he gave her his total love.

Sheila O'Hare

MY ELEGY
(A cyclist's elegy)

When this life I leave,
Please don't worry, please don't grieve.
Scatter my ashes along my favourite byway,
Then at night, in peace under the
Hedgerows I'll lay.

By dawn's early light I'll see the farmer
Sowing his field,
I'll still be there when he gathers
The crops they yield.

In the autumn when withered brown leaves
Are falling,
Friends awheel may imagine me calling.
And as they ride by,
I'll be among the grit that always gets
Into someone's eyes.

In the winter I'll be mixed in with the
Ice, snow, frost, and dirt,
But of course me, this will not hurt.

In the spring will come warm, fresh rain,
Freeing me from the soil again.

In the summer I'll be turned back to
Ash and dust,
And borne on high in a windy gust.

Bardon

THE ANGEL'S LAMENT

He is dead . . . the man whose wretched soul I was sent to watch!
It was my portion, my extreme duty to persevere with his soul . . .
And I did my duty . . . I spoke to him earnestly, by day and by night.
I encouraged every good thought . . . I praised every good deed.
I was with him, even at the end, when he departed this life alone
And no human hand was there to console him or share the Gospel.
He was a fearful soul, timid, withdrawn, indeed, truly lonely.
All through his childhood he was bullied, victimised, abused.
Alas, he chose not to forgive . . . nor to seek God out from then on.
I mourn for him, fellow angels, yet his heart grew cold and hard.
I spoke to him in his dreams, urged him to seek the higher path,
The nobler path, the perfect path to Paradise, but all to no avail!
I wept for him the day he was closest to the Kingdom of Christ:
Billy Graham's radio sermon filled his room with hopes of salvation,
Forgiveness of sins, courage and determination to fight for Jesus!
And I alone saw the man wrestle with the truth, agonising what to do.
Would he at last respond, seek the Saviour's salvation, climb Calvary?
I knelt beside him in prayer pleading with the Lord of Lords!
I wept for him: so alone, so fearful, so torn in his spirit, so lost!
But I witnessed his heart grow cold and hard once more . . .
He never tuned in again - Church and Christianity were dismissed . . .
He poured out his heart to no man, woman or child . . .
Thus, he knew nothing of true love or sacrifice or blessing,
Nor offered one word of praise to the Father, the Son and the Spirit!
Thus the Devil played with him, treated his soul as if it were a toy!
Fellow angels, you know how it could have been so different!
This wretched soul could have blossomed like the desert rose!
He could have been saved, become a preacher, saved millions of souls!
If only, if only, if only he repented, asked the Father's forgiveness!
He could have been saved, alas, not so, not so, and so I weep for him.

Denis Martindale

IRON SURVIVOR

Oh my dead spirit
That still within me lies
Tho' my body lives on
'Tis unable to compromise

I was so alive
The iron survivor
But England's rogues dug so
Intensely, not giving up either

Oh murderers now
Do you not fear I'll haunt
You wrecked my self-esteem
Know my memory will taunt

Always behind you
I'm your personal ghost
This you did make me and
You must now feel the pain you hoist

Tearing me apart
Spirit separated
Satisfied then you were
Now you live breath abated

For I'll be lifted
New breath breathed within
Okay, you broke me
But now you can watch me win.

Barbara Sherlow

QUEENIE

Dying eyes, dull and tired, begin to close,
to court the joys of life no more.
Shallow breaths of laboured pain,
bemoan the anguish of unwilling death.
She looks to me,
and I to her,
a begging stare of little hope.
A moment I will carry to my own grave.

She tasks me with her saddened face,
and questions why I do not help.
I can do nothing but sit,
and pray.

And cry.

An empty silence,
beckoning the end,
her body still, portends the onset of decay.
She leaves me quietly, destiny complete,
her last breath a whisper in my mind.
Gentle heart of many years,
now tends the beat of lasting sleep.

My heart is heavy, orphaned by its loss,
loyalty and love, that cannot be replaced.
Widowed of my soul, I cry a tear,
a tribute to undying love.
I hold her in my trembling arms,
and wrap her lovingly,
a shrouding of my memories.

I look once more upon her face,
a victim of unwelcome end.
A lonely spirit stares me back,
and in that moment, I too,
am dead.

Lawrence Mentesh

You And I In The Promised Land

(For Pauline Jones, in memory of her dear son)

Walk with me on the tarnished road,
Potholed and broken with sadness,
Burdened with a loss that is more
Than words can ever say.
I see your shoulders weighed down
With a sorrow I bear myself.

I say these words in love
That you may know comfort and healing:
The Lord bless you and keep you,
May be make his face to shine upon you,
Be gracious to you, and give you peace.
Amen.

For now we must rest in hope,
That firm and solid anchor of the faith,
Until we see our loved ones again,
One day beyond time, in the kingdom.
So hard is the way, we stumble and fall,
Cut and hurt ourselves, even when we do right.

May the Lord think often of you,
You who are the called according to his purpose.
All things may work together to our good,
But at times I can scarcely credit it.
How I wish you had never been tried
By such a hard providence.

The ten plagues of Egypt had an end.
Those terrible, majestic signs and wonders
Of an almighty, caring Father's hand.
He will lead you through the waters
Of a stormy flood-gorged Nile,
Until your feet touch the dry land of Canaan.

Broken heart not mended, still walk with me.
We know the way the Evangelist points.
Ever onward and upward on our hard narrow path,
Struggling daily to do what is just and right,
Looking for the resurrection of the dead
And the life to come, Amen.

David Tallach

PLANET

You are the storm on Jupiter,
The blood stains swirling
Over the mighty mass.
You are turbulent red,
Swimming circles in yourself,
You're the storm overhead
Which will never pass.
You're a full moon
In my stomach
On a sky of turquoise blue,
And I hope you can forgive me,
Baby daughter,
I love you.

Erin Halliday

THE GARDENER

Last year those autumn leaves
had barely hit the ground
when up he'd jump.
And with a mighty blower bought one Christmas
blast them from his sight.
The weeds would never grow
between the bushes.
Grasped by gentle hands
   they'd find themselves uprooted
     - cast aside to grow again elsewhere

Last year the fruit trees bowed beneath their load
of tasty succulent green berries.
Carefully protected from the predator.
We ate our fill - and more
  and gave the neighbours pies
    and jam in jars.

Tonight the sky's too clear
and soon the frost will creep across those fallen leaves.
The lawn uncut, unruly now
will sparkle as it hardens fast on every blade.
The bushes, stripped by tiny claws
will yield afresh their scars to icy fingers.
Unswept paths - a testimony to that much heard adage
'Time moves on'
And this year though we ache with deepest sadness
  still we face it
    that the gardener has gone
      and no
        he won't return!

Jo Wood

THE LITTLE BRONZE GIRL OF REGENT'S PARK

I wonder who the model was for her,
The once so pretty, vital, rustic maid?
What was her voice, her nature, to infer
To be immortalised in bronze, embayed
Back in Victorian times, but not at all
Victorian, dressed for a gayer clime.
Shading her eyes, she stands upon a wall
And looks for me across the gulf of time,
- Or so I like to fancy. Was she Jean,
Elspeth, Lavinia, or an unknown name?
Perhaps she was a Sally, or a Jo,
A milkmaid, seamstress, weaver, all the same
Exactly who she was I'll never know.
So charming as she is in bronze, forever young,
What was she like in truth? Would I could endow
With some Pygmalion power, her life, her tongue,
Her form, her feelings, to come smiling now.

A J Vogel

WWWILL THIS BE *IT?*

Some five or six decades ago,
faint flickering lines on tiny screen
enthralled a small elite, just so.
Without TV, what might have been?

'Tis said that conversation ceased,
transfixed before the magic eye.
Relationships, once rife, decreased;
Blighted by 'The Box' - to die.

The nightly pilgrimage became
a day-long ardour nation-wide;
Ensconced before a flickering frame
forever focused - 'Telecide'

Some sixty years have now elapsed;
A new addiction looms on line.
The 'Net' is cast! Will all be grasped?
Downloaded, digital decline.

Eternally enmeshed - E-mail;
Now links the world in far-flung place.
Society sits in isolation,
no longer meeting face to face.

Lament those long-gone days of old,
when quill and paper carried news;
Affairs of heart, liaisons bold,
when people met to air their views.

The world wide web, a prison cell;
where condemned surf in isolation.
This Elegy for those who dwell
commemorates the 'E-torn' nation.

Gerald S Bell

In Memory Of Harold

My parents split up
When I was very small.
Then, Harold came along
And adopted us all.

He filled the role
Of my father well,
And made a home out
Of a childhood hell.

For many years to come
Harold seemed okay.
But then his world
Suddenly turned to grey.

His relentless illness
Spread so very fast.
I never thought that day
Would be our last.

He looked so gaunt
And stripped of good cheer.
Hiding behind his eyes -
The sadness and fear.

And I remember
How much I cried
That sad day my
Stepfather died.

I cherish the many
Moments we both shared,
And in his heart
He knew how much we all cared.

Peter Steele

THE WHISTLER
(Dedicated to Fred Howard)

You whistled a tune, from morn till noon,
Enjoying your trek to the town and back.
A happier person, you never did see,
Hardly believing you were ninety-three.

With the world of steam, you spent most of your days,
Railway stations, with blotted out rays.
Passenger comfort was your main concern,
Every day different, with something to learn.

A slower pace then, those days in time,
Now modern expresses, thunder down the line.
Memories recalled, had me truly enthralled.
A life on the fast track, but no going back.

A friendship was forged, when we met that day,
But five years gone on now, since you've passed away.
The journey you travelled, is now at an end,
With angels to guide you, round every bend.

A lovely man, with a heart of gold,
Waistcoated, and white hat to keep out the cold.
I remember your laughter, and kindness to me,
Still wrapped in my thoughts, and given for free.

Janice Thorogood

ELSA'S ELEGY

You were lent to us for one short year,
The cost to you was dear,
We could not tame your feline spirit,
Which shone out loud and clear.

You paid the price for independence,
On one of your hunting trips,
By crossing the road you paid the ultimate price,
Though you lingered on for a few more days.

Our only hope was that the vet could ease your pain,
Our prayers were not enough to bring you back to us,
Our life without you, dear, wild, captivating and bewitching
Elsa, will never be quite the same again.

You will never know how much we loved you,
You filled our life, with your joy of life,
You will always have a special place,
Elsa, deep inside of us.

On reaching your spiritual home,
May a new joy be found
And that your release from pain,
Will take you on high to a happier hunting ground.

We will never forget you however long,
You filled our days with your attitude,
But what wouldn't we give?
To see you, dear dynamic Elsa, alive once more.

Mary Lawson

TO SOMEONE WHO'S JUST LOST A PARTNER

Pain is no stranger to my day
Woe is not alien to my heart,
But that time's taken love away
Has torn my weary soul apart;
I know with life, there's always hope,
The spirit lives eternally,
But with you I could live, and cope
With all that life would throw at me:

Why must a loved one though be left
When death has brought their partner peace,
Why leave a cherished soul bereft
Of any hope that grief may cease?
I would not want you suffering
To keep your spirit by my side,
But why must destiny so sting
A broken heart that weeps inside?

I take great comfort though, that soon
Will precious life in death decline,
Then I once more can hum the tune
That tells you that you're loved and mine;
Wait on sweet love, in Heaven's sway
I'll join you when my time is done,
It won't be long till come our way
The time our souls combine as one.

Nicholas Winn

ALONG LIFE'S ROAD

We move along, we move along
Along life's road our favourite song, our favourite song.
Happy as the years go by, the years go by
The happy years of you and I, of you and I.

Our favourite walks along life's way
The special flowers, the special days,
We shared the laughter and the tears
Our anniversary, birthdays, years.

We move along, we move along
Along life's road, our favourite song, our favourite song
We thought our days would always last
As our winter summer days then passed.

Then suddenly you are gone from me
Now the desolate days now that I can see, I can see
I move along, I move along
Along life's road now empty long.

How long the road without you here
My saddened heart, the saddened tears
Now in my heart sweet memory
The deepest love you gave to me.

Now in the shelter of my heart, you're there
In the shelter of my heart, I care, I care, oh how I care
In my dreams I hold you tight,
Then reality of the day, the light.

I wake, I realise I cannot see
Now the warmth of your sweet memory now comforts me
In the shelter of my heart, in the shelter of my heart
I hold you close to me, oh so near, so very, very near.

The memory of you I revere, I revere
Oh how I cherish your memory
In the shelter of my heart you're near to me
Oh so very near, so very, very near.

A King

THE LAST ROSE OF SUMMER

In those foggy waking moments
'I think you'd better listen to the news!'
rasped a voice filled with urgency
rudely the radio interrupted my still slumbering
cobwebs of confusion; disbelief clawed my throat
in a vice-like grip as truth slowly dawned.
Now the world is stationary
as we watched mourners laying living flowers
at Kensington Palace . . .
but the flowers drooped in a veil of tears
the sun eclipsed
a light extinguished
on 31st August 1997.
Disbelief dispelled to reality
your life was transitory
tragic, fragmented
you flew too close to the cutting edge,
an icon of stunning beauty but a fox on the run
till - there was nowhere else to run
except escaping from paparazzi and the press
trapped by the four bittersweet winds of N-E-W-S
a press prison.

The winds of change are here to stay
features soften on TV
news presenters spread shockwaves
but - yes it's true - you are dramatically
dead. Disbelief claws.

I won't forget your care, charisma,
charm and beauty.
Most of all your laughter
hiding the struggle within
just to be *you*
masking a million tears
through memory's mists
we see through a glass darkly.
We will never know why you had to go
but your memory will burn in our hearts
like a candle which can
never be extinguished
in a wild howling wind.
Farewell, Diana.

Judy Studd

Unexpected Guest An Elegy To My Brother

The funeral is over,
the mourners have all gone.
How many days dear brother
since you walked in the sun.

As death so quietly stealing
takes one we love and know
and leaves the family grieving
when our tears begin to flow.

Our hearts are filled with sadness;
the loss so hard to bear,
but we know dearest brother
you are now in God's safe care.

How many days dear brother
since you walked in the sun
and left us feeling sorrow
for your work here is done:
But happily for you dear
a new life has begun.

Ruth Barclay Brook

ELEGY
(In loving memory of Alan Henry)

An open sky, aquamarine blue. Tranquillity and silence.
Nothing to disturb the peace of summer.
The portal to eternity, with neither a wing to lift,
nor a drop of rain to put us asunder.
Such is the triumph of your peaceful spirit, your gentle way,
that it will always remind me of summer.
Yet, this peace which is deeper, purer, more everlasting
than the seasons,
marks you out as a person of such endearing human qualities
as to make you exceptional in this age.
Someone in whom one could place trust without it becoming a burden,
for whom no extra task was too much,
who never spoke ill of others, and who often laughed.
I once described you as 'the hand that rocks the cradle'.
The season of caring was never over for you.
You were a strong staff that offered itself to be leant on
without breaking,
but that nevertheless had branches and flowers
which filled with dancing butterflies and birds,
and roots which sunk deep into the Scottish earth,
and which drunk of the love of your kith and kin;
A love which feeds us on heaven still,
or shows us what heaven might be.

Linda Anne Landers

My Neighbour's Cat

My neighbour's cat is a dear little soul,
I work hard in the garden, then he digs a hole!
He knows that I am a really good friend,
I don't get angry; so the rules he'll bend.
But, I tell him, fine earth is for seeds and veg,
He must do what he has to, behind the hedge!
My neighbour's cat hides beside the tree,
Then suddenly jumps out - to frighten me,
He whizzes by, as I kneel on the ground,
Darts up a tree, as if chased by a hound.
He pauses now and then, to have a chat -
I talk to him, you see, about this and that!
This friend of mine has a sister too,
Who also thinks that my garden's her loo!
She chases the butterflies, moths and bees -
And scares the birds up in the trees.
My neighbour's cat nips in, when I open the door,
And in winter he lies by the fire, on the floor.
But in the garden, for now, he can snooze or play,
Because, for me, he makes it a happier day.

Jeannette Kelly

CAT

Cat moves -
In precision
Through the fears of your mind:
Cat's an image in the stillness -
And a moment in time.
Cat waits -
Tense
Poised on the stair,
Fresh from the smell
Of her daytime lair.
Cat listens -
Close
Her shadow by a light,
- Prying green eyes
Pierce the void of the night.
Cat's a mirage -
A face
Drawn on the wall,
A conscious formation
You cannot recall.

Michael Tinker

ROBBIE - ANIMAL RESCUE

Our Robbie is a Westie
Just a babe in arms,
What wicked ways these Westies have
They certainly have their charms.

He loves to come and kiss you
As to say 'Come on let's go'
Another day dawns with the same routine
How he loves you so.

A brush, a romp, a walk and play,
Another beginning to a perfect day,
And when the day is over
And those eyes begin to close
We'll do the same routine tomorrow
Because Robbie's our little rose.

Scottie

IN MEMORY OF ABI

(Aged 9 months)

From the midst of mourning came
A small promise of tomorrow
Iron bars surrounded you - victim of an obdurate breed.
Yet your innocence infused upon our sorrow;
In an instant a bond implied
No more concrete floors, nor feeling of abandonment.

Here amongst a friendly strain you blossomed before our eyes
Time lay at your side, a legacy of your youth.
Oh, balmy days of woodland trod,
Oh, nights of comfort shared.
A kindred spirit honoured and understood.
Yet, oh so cruel life, who came again to slay,
Sweet virgin as she lay; complete in her trust of man.
Oh, hapless creature how still are you disposed -

A latent executioner, released with gaseous breath
And the legacy is nought but wasted -
Once again our fragile happiness is exposed
And from the ashes emerges - once more desolate heart.

Sleep long and well dear friend - wait for me.

Therese Muchewicz

JENNY'S CAT

I live in the country and have a good home
With a garden to play in, and fields to roam.
My real name is Tiddles and I answer to that
But I'm known to most people as Jenny's cat
I try to look fierce as I crouch on my tum
And wait by the gate for wild beasts to come
But the family all laugh and say look at that
Then I know I'm no Tiger, just Jenny's cat.
I sneak upstairs and jump on the bed
I snuggle up close and push out old ted.
But I'm hustled downstairs in two minutes flat
To the basket provided for Jenny's cat.
I often go hunting to catch mice and voles.
Well I am chief inspector of all mouse holes.
Then I bring back an offering to put on the mat.
A nice little present to Jenny from her cat.

J Noble

ASPIE - BELOVED CAT

Tiny toes and stripy tail,
'Where's my food?' we'd hear you wail,
'I am here make room for me,
I like it curled up on your knee.

I think I need to pay a call,
I'll just nip out across the wall
Where are my pals? I want to play,
I haven't seen 'Polo' today!

I'm feeling tired, been here so long,
I'm really old, and not so strong.
Farewell my family, see you soon,
Be happy for me, heaven's a boon.'

Dawn A Taylor

OUR RUE

We have a dog, his name is Rue
He makes us laugh, with things he do

He is half King Charles and half Jack Russell
But he's no nipper and doesn't need a muzzle

Jack's in his hind quarters, but have a Charlie face
He'd never win medals for running a race

He is black and white, but got brown ears
Children love him, they have no fears

At eighteen months old, he's our baby boy
To all the family, he is such a joy

The children walk him, taking scoop and bag
They know he's pleased, as his tail will wag

He watches the children as they leave for school
And the time they come home, as he's no fool

His favourite meal is a dish of chicken
When the dish is empty, he keeps lickin'

He's got his dog bed, but prefers Dad's chair
Even Dad will leave him, and sit elsewhere

He loves to be brushed, and have a cuddle
With ball or toy he tries to juggle

He barks quite loud, when there's a knock on the door
If it's a friend, he'll hold out his paw

But when it's a stranger, he gets up and prowl
If he's not too sure, he gives a small growl

We also have a beautiful black cat
They wash each other, as they lay on the mat

To us he's the best dog to have ever been found
We wouldn't sell him for a million pound

Violet Crisp

BRANDY GREY OF HOWDLES

He is no duke or fox which people could mock,
He was a little runt when he was first born,
A funny little fur ball which rolled around the lawn.
Black as a sheep or grey as a wolf,
Brandy Grey is the little lamb of the west which is the best.
He likes to leap or jump in the fields of yellow.
My Brandy Grey is a caring fellow,
Who knows when to stoop.
When feelings are low he knows who to look after,
Or even to go to warm them with his fur.
Comforting and kind my dog respects me all the time.
Brandy Grey of Howdles I'm glad you're mine.
For forever and all the time.

Joanne Reynolds (15)

LITTLE JACKIE RUSSELL

Little Jackie Russell she causes some trouble
Her barking just drives me insane
She pulls on her lead when she goes for a walk
It's her territory, the long stony lane
She's a quart in a pint pot, a rat on long legs
She snaps when anyone gets near
Yet she's loveable and cuddly, intelligent and bubbly
But the hoover still fills her with fear
She looks like a puppy, an intelligent yuppie
Roast chicken is her favourite food
She gets under the covers, usually her mother's
To sulk when she gets in a mood
She's just like her owner, a grumbler and groaner
The needle is high on my list
The thought of no barking or snapping or snarling
Is something I've often wished.

So watch it!

Lindsey Metcalfe

MY JACK RUSSELL

While I am writing my poem,
I peep down at my dog,
She's lying across my feet,
And feels like a log.

She loves to be near me,
And worships me so,
She's my best companion,
She loves me I know.

She goes for her lead
And brings it to me,
She wiggles her tail,
And she's full of glee.

We set out in the cold
And hurry along.
She pulls me so fast
She is so very strong.

She keeps close beside me
We walk for miles,
Up hill and down dale,
Even climb over stiles.

My Jack Russell and I arrive home
We are ready for our bed.
A drink, her favourite chocolate
And then she lays down her head.

M Wheatley

TIGER CAT

Lying in the long grass like a solitary tiger,
Poised to pounce, eyes open, just a little bit.
The fur is hidden, the ears pricked and waiting,
The end result is nothing to catch today,
Nothing to chase until the evening,
Maybe a small brown shrew, a baby bird will fall,
Nothing to watch but butterflies, winged insects,
I can see them all.

Waiting in the grass like a tiger pausing,
Poised to pounce, eyes open, just a little bit.
The ears are up, the senses waiting,
The end result is nothing to catch today,
Nothing to see until at midnight,
Maybe a hunting mouse, something then to do,
Nothing to give but a warning, here in the grass,
I am waiting for you.

Christine Lacey

FLUFFY'S DAY OUT

Rebecca has a rabbit
Fluffy is it's name
She wanted to take it to school
But Fluffy wasn't tame

When she tried to lift it up
It barked just like a dog
Bit her on the arm
Then ran into the bog

It hopped upon the window sill
Barked once more
Then leaped towards the door
Rebecca failed to catch it
'Cause her arm was sore

Jordan joined in the fun
Then they chased the little bun
They cornered it in the living room
Fluffy now had met her doom

A final hop towards the door
Jordan spread out on the floor
Rebecca caught it by the tail
Now Fluffy's back inside her jail.

Jim Nicol

A Cat's Tale

A cat on our fence was a stray without doubt,
Someone somewhere had kicked it out.
It looked so scruffy, so hungry and scared
What a shame no one cared.
I got some meat and milk from the fridge,
That empty tummy I must abridge.
I opened our door to offer the meal,
But in a flash all I saw was its heel.
I put the food down, came in and shut the door,
I peeped through the window and then in a jot,
The cat came back and scoffed the lot.
This ritual continued every night
The cat ate and drank it its heart's delight.
Although I am so good, it won't let me get near
It spits and claws at me, it's so full of fear.
Bit by bit I moved its meals nearer to our door,
Then I finally put it inside the open door.
The cat came in and ate the food, then took a little peep,
It jumped up on a cosy chair, curled up and went to sleep.
We left drink and food and litter tray, before we went to bed,
Next day the cat has a bite to eat, then followed my husband to the shed.
It strolled around the garden, and watched the goldfish in the pool,
After lying on the lawn it cleaned up its fur, this cat's no fool.
It chose our home, when it was down and out,
Now it knows the comforts and is free to roam about.
We have learned to love it, with its lovely coat and stance
It's been twelve months since we took it in
And gave it a second chance.

Dorothy Groom

TERRY

I feel so very sad today -
My favourite friend has gone away.
Up to Heaven she softly flew,
Within the light of the morning dew.

I feel so very sad that she has gone away,
No more we'll romp and tumble amongst the new-mown hay,
No more within the tractor, together we all will ride,
No more within the truck, she'll ever sit with pride.

She was my one and only, friend forever true.
Her memory I'll treasure, within my mind anew.
And when one day we meet, within that heavenly place,
I know we'll both have joy, each written o'er our face.

So until then dear Terry, a grave for you we've made,
Words 'Rest in Peace' upon a cross, and flowers there we've laid.
I'll love you forever - and I know my dad will too.
So wait for us in Heaven, till we come and visit you.

E J Sherwood

JAKE 1984 - 1996

Thank you Jake for spending your life with us.
You were the sweetest thing.
So full of character, so full of love,
You found a place in all our hearts.
And you'll be there forever,
To make us laugh and make us cry.
Such a beautiful boy - we'll miss you.

K Sinclair-Thomson

A CHILD'S BEST FRIEND

As I get home from my school
It's you I want to see
You're asleep in your bed
But you wake to look at me

We then go into the garden
Where I throw a ball for you
I then laugh and smile
At the silly things you do

Round and round you go
Trying to catch your tail
If I leave the garden
You jump over the rail

Then you follow me down the street
To play with me and my friends
You make us all so happy
We hope this never ends.

Wayne Carr

FURBLE

A weight of worries makes me sigh
As I come in through the door
But the welcome trill and the shining eyes
Make my drooping spirits soar.

It's as if a living ray of sun
Has lifted all the gloom
As she steps on velvet slippered paws
To dance across the room.

Her tail, a banner black and gold
Weaves magic round my feet
And all my troubles melt away
As my dear friend I greet.

And when at night I fail to sleep
For worry, pain or guilt
She'll make me laugh by pouncing
On my feet beneath the quilt!

She knows my feelings, understands
And my life would be much duller
Without my long-haired Furble
And her coat of many colours.

G M Zambonini

MY PET HAMSTER

Poppy is my pet,
And sometimes needs a vet,
As she rolls in her ball,
She rams into the wall.

Poppy does not make a sound,
But you know when she is around,
In her car she bounds,
She gives your feet a pound.

Poppy comes running when you call,
And does gymnastics on ladders so tall,
It's a wonder she does not fall.

From pink little nose to stubby little tail,
You cannot fail to fall in love with this cute hamster female.

Rebecca Lee (9)

MY BEST MATES

Rainy days and cloudy skies
Then I'll look into your eyes
You cheer me up and make me giggle
Especially when your bottoms wiggle!

You love your walkies in the park
Where around the trees you leave your mark
I love the way you tails are curly
But do we really have to get up so early?

Playing catch, chasing around the table
On digging the lawn - you're both very able
Dancing, playing, woo-ooing your silly chants
It's like living with a couple of elephants!

You're cuddly, loving, loud and proud
And always attract an inquisitive crowd
'No, they're not huskies!' I always say
You'd rather eat ice-cream than pull a sleigh!

I dread the days when you're no longer here
But let me make just one thing clear
Nothing lifts my spirits higher
Than my gorgeous Akitas, Anouk and Kaia!

Karen May-Seymour

HOT DAY

White,
White whiskered
So polite
When from the night
You return,
Cold and wet
To brush my bare untrousered leg
In thanks for meagre plateful
Poured quickly from the jug
That sits half filled

Then, sated, to the door
With outstretched paw
You ask that freedom be returned
The early morning grey
Holds promise of a day
Of feline pleasure
Of wait and watch
And dart and pounce

But soon as clouds roll back and sun returns
The pace is slowed, and slowed, and turns
To torpid, languid, slothful rest
Hot slabs provide the bed
On which you roll and soak the rays
That melt your bones
Is this the best
That day of days
When you recall
Those tropic ways
Buried in your ancestry?

T R Jebb

To A Foundling Puppy

Where did you come from.
Did you just stray.
Or were you abandoned
in a most callous way.

You've got a golden head
and a white speckled nose.
Long brown legs
with white tips
on their toes.

A deep white chest
that boldly sticks out
like a lifeguard on duty
of that, there's no doubt.

Tender brown eyes
that twinkle with fun.
Especially when off
to the park for a run.

You frisk and bark
at the girls and the boys.
And then for a lark
you run off with their toys.

Then home for a feed
and feeling quite snoozy.
You creep in to bed
my dear little Susie.

May Richardson

A Poem For Tiggie

Devoted is Tiggie to me and me him
When I open the door he is there with arched back
And standing on tiptoes

When dinner is served he sits on the table
And is completely satisfied when able to sample just a morsel

When his brush is produced he is not so keen
But tends to grin and bare it if only for me

His eyes stare and blink and tired he becomes
And heads for my bed for his place amongst the teddies

Tiggie is proud and admires himself in the mirrors
And right too as he is rather the most handsome cat

For Tiggie loves me and I love Tiggie

Moira Clelland

ON THE DEATH OF A MUCH LOVED DOG

*(In loving memory of my darling Prince,
died December 22nd 1973, aged 12 years)*

No-one knows, my love,
Just how much I miss you.
From time to time I shed
A silent tear,
But in a dark and quiet room
Where no-one else
My sad notes will hear.

It is no easy thing
To decide which course to take,
But I could not let you suffer -
I had no right.
Within my heart I knew
I could not keep you here.
I am so sad tonight.

Hazel Carroll

THANK YOU TESS

When I was a girl we looked after Tess
She was very good, never made a mess.
A beautiful German Shepherd was she,
And I loved her - and for a time she loved me,
Just for a week she was mine to adore,
I knew it was wrong to wish for more,
And when she went home I secretly cried,
'If only she were mine' I wistfully sighed.
But now in my own home and a woman grown
I have Zelda to love, yes a dog of my own,
To give unconditional love right to the end,
My German Shepherd, devoted friend.

Norma Washbrook

A BUSY DAY FOR TOM CAT

Lazy ginger Tom cat dozing in the sun,
keeping half an eye on whatever strolls by.
You sleep when you want and eat when you please,
the only problem that you have, is a handful of fleas.
The birdies all hate you, but you know you're great,
you get more dinner than you need on your plate.
We all love you - more than you love us,
in fact, it wouldn't bother you if you got no fuss.
You look at us like fools and live by your own rules.
Life's complete - when you're king of all the street.

Amanda Averies

ANIMAL CRACKERS

I used to be a zookeeper, but the elephant stood on my toe.
Why the stupid mutt did that, I will never know.
I was transferred to the lions, but got locked inside the cage,
I had my left arm ripped off by a lion in a rage.
I thought the monkeys were harmless, but much to my surprise,
One crept up to me when I wasn't looking and poked me in the eye.
I have partial vision in one eye, but at least I have got two,
The spitting cobra got me in the other eye, I don't know what to do.
The boss said try the rabbits, they're docile most of the time,
I was only with them a day or two when to my horror I did find,
When I went to stroke a pregnant doe, the vicious little blighter
Went and bit off two fingers, well at least I am a little lighter.
I had two dozen stitches in my purple, swollen hand,
But to top it all, from the animals I have been banned.

Don Goodwin

ROWAN

(Rowan is an Estrela, Portuguese Mountain Dog, measuring 30" at the shoulder)

I have an adolescent dog who doesn't want his food.
The vet says it's his hormones, put him in a funny mood.
The tablets she prescribed for him should make him want to eat,
But giving them's a problem that has really got me beat.

Some food he goes and plays with, which he tosses high and low
Or spits it out or only sniffs and doesn't want to know.
Just sit him down and take his jaws then tell him, 'Open wide.'
Is what you're thinking I should do to pop them well inside.

He's eel-like when I try it and there's no way any force
Opens up the clenched-fast teeth of this dog, strong as a horse.
Mortar and pestle's worth a try with sausage, fish or cheese
To bind the grounds together so he'll swallow them with ease.

To no avail this trickery, eating has no reason
When all this dog has on his mind is a bitch in season.
This 'catch 22' situation's very hard to beat -
To make him eat a tablet, he's to have to make him eat!

Hazel M Stanley

OUR PET

Our pet was very special to us
He's no longer here and we feel so sad.
He was a dog that we found as a stray
And he followed us round like a shadow all day.

Perhaps he was young when thrown out to the world
Veterinary said his age about a year,
Very house-trained - must have had a home
We cannot believe he was just left to roam.

It took some time for love to grow
As we knew by his ways he'd been badly abused.
We gave all our love and he returned it to us
And soon there was just perfect trust.

Eleven years together we had
Our lives were changed from that very first day
A wonderful dog and such a friend,
Still cannot believe it had to end.

Quite a large dog as Alsatians are,
When put to sleep we carried him home in the car.
We loved that dog with all our heart
Which broke that day we had to part.

At peace in our garden he is near we feel
And hope in time our minds will heal.
What would we have missed if we had turned him away
On that fateful day when we found a stray.

K M Hook

MY BEAUTIFUL CAT

My beautiful cat was a rescued mog,
Came with friends one November fog,
Rescued from the depths of deep despair
To discover the comfort of a favourite chair
Or the fireside soft, warm mat
And then there's Mother's favourite hat.
Common domestic breed I'm told,
But to me, he's pure gold.
Long, sleek fur in black and white
I never let him out of sight.
A purrfect gentleman, very refined,
No impurrfections on his mind.
Birds, spiders and flies come in some days,
Good day says Tim and sends them on their ways.
All God's creatures, big and small,
He loves them and He made them all.
I named him Timmy, nothing posh,
But you should see him have a wash.
Groomed to purrfection every day
Sits up in front as if to say
'Here I am, washed, clean and ready.
Help! Watch out! The brush, be steady.'
My beautiful cat is a great big treasure,
More valuable than any wealth can measure.

Timmy's Owner

MY COMPANION

He looks at me with baleful eyes
And gives a long, sad sigh
Then walks from me with head held high.
Can I help it if no longer
I can sit right here and ponder.
You've sat with me an hour
In this comfortable bower
But now my dear, I must get on
With all those household chores anon.
And you my little pussycat
Must curl up on some comfy mat.

Shirley Morgan

HOPE

It was just another day
I was cooking another dinner in the ordinary way
The telephone rang, just another ring
I could not speak, I just had to pray
Please don't leave me, don't just go.

We are mates, we hang out together
But you already know.
Yes, you are a cat named George
But with a human touch,
With your brown, striped coat and handsome face.
A bit of a lad with the girls and all that
By the way, can you hear me?
I do hope so.
I tried for you, but the answer was 'no'.

Do you remember when you were a kitten
And your ears and paws didn't fit
Because they were too big?
I thought we'd be together forever, you and me.

Now I will say goodbye
Until I pass your way
On this extraordinary day.

Pamela Hawkins

WHISKY

She lies stretched out, head on paws,
Watching as I go through the doors.
Then I put on shoes, pick up her lead,
To say, 'walkies,' there is no need.
Quick as a flash, she cannot wait
Till I lock the door and open the gate.
Soon, we reach the fields and beck
And all I see is just a speck
As she wanders through the tall grass
Sniffing at everything; nothing she'll pass.
She'll meet a dog, friend or foe.
If not friend, then off she'll go
Looking for interesting things to see,
To roll in the grass, have fun, be free.
Then home again, a nice cool drink,
And she's sound asleep, quick as a wink.

Doris E Barrow

REX

(Dedicated to our rescued Dobermann)

You came to us with special needs
A dog of suffering you were indeed.
Your eyes lifeless and dead,
Ears severed but erect on your head.
A body crippled and deformed you had
From beatings by people more than bad.

Your first days with us we remember well,
Warm bed, food, love, no more living hell.
Nostrils twitched with thrill of scented air,
Be it pheasant, rabbit or retreating hare.
Our only haunt which we knew from the start
Was your failing heart which caused us to part.

Three wonderful years we had with you,
Regaining your love and trust in humans too.
Days on the beach daring seagulls to land,
On surrounding rocks, water and sand.
Fields, hills and moors your heaven you found,
Your favourite digging rabbit holes deep in the ground.

Then came the day you didn't look right,
Looked with eyes that said every breath was a fight.
The vet was right you must never again
Suffer confusion, neglect or pain.
With all our strength we stayed with you
We'd made a promise, the least we could do.

In my arms you rested your head,
Closed your eyes, then you were dead.
Your ashes we scattered on your favourite beach
And from this poem we hope we'll teach
To rescue a dog, no matter how long,
Takes dedication, love till the end, then be strong.

Gillian Holt

BENGY (COCKER SPANIEL)

That was a day I will never forget
That final long journey down to the vet

All the family's farewells were said
How could I tell you what lay ahead?

You gave the vet your little paw
And then sank slowly to the floor

Your bed's still there and so are your toys
But so are the memories of happiness and joy

Those desperate years spent on the dole
That's when you were my heart and soul

Down to the beach pulling on your lead
And into the water at great speed

Into the car all soaking wet
Those are the times I won't forget

So sleep well my faithful friend
To you and me it's not the end

Night, night, it's time for bed.

James William Page

TOBY

Back door's open Toby, out you go,
No I don't care if there's snow.
Toby, Toby, get off the soil
In the garden I have to toil.
Toby please keep off the flowers
And come on in boy, it's going to shower.
Finished Toby let's wipe your feet
Toby boy you are so sweet.
Settle down Toby by the fire
All that romping you must be tired.
You're a rascal, a scamp, anyone can see
But you're my little Yorkie and my company.

Elizabeth Spiller

DOGMAN

If my dog were a person, I think he'd be the sort of chap
Who'd wear braces with his trousers and a checked flat cap.
He'd keep his hands in his pockets and he'd always smile at you,
And he'd doff his cap in greeting and he'd simply say 'How do!'
He'd stride around whistling and always take his time,
The day would always be pleasant and the sun would always shine.
He'd stop and talk to everyone, and shake hands whenever they'd meet
And he'd find the simplest things in life always the biggest treat.
He'd be welcoming to everyone, young and old, friend or strange,
Except of course the milkman (I don't see why that should change).
The ones he wasn't sure about he would just ignore,
He'd sit out on his step and warn them from his door.
But mostly, he'd be laid back and eager to please.
Maybe a bit of a joker. *Maybe* a bit of a tease.
He wouldn't bother about TV or cars or phones or such.
Yes, if he were a person, I think I'd like him just as much.
Content, relaxed and happy. Easy going and free.
(Of course, if he *were* a person, his best mate would be me!)

S P Oldham

AZURE EYES

As I enter the room, the first thing I see
Is two pairs of blue eyes looking towards me -
I, smiling a welcome; warm, polite;
One other more wary, a creature of the night.

Companions for each other, on the bed they lie
I get to know them both as the months go by.
The lady, ill in bed; I was never to see her rise
And her Siamese cat, with the blue, blue eyes.

Neighbours come and go, visitors abound,
The cat stays on the bed, making not a sound.
Silently she lies, keeping guard; just sharing;
Giving her particularly feline brand of caring.

Smooth fur beneath the hand; a gentle rhythmic purr;
Such small comforts as the day begins to blur.
One pair of bright blue eyes is the last thing that she sees -
Her Siamese cat Azure, with eyes blue as the sea.

Julie C Ashton

READY TO RUN

Lying in the garden, soaking up the sun,
My legs are twitching, ready to run.
I'm chasing rabbits up and downhill,
Nearly catching them, oh what a thrill.
Almost got them, just across the stream,
'What's that noise?' Oh . . . it was only a dream.
Lie back down, eyes shut tight,
Shielding them from the bright sunlight.
But cats beware, I'm not really asleep,
Quick as a flash at you I'll leap.
One of these days as you cross my path,
I'll get you, I will and have the last laugh.
But oh, it's such a terrible fate,
That you sit there, smirking, outside my gate.
My mistress is calling, I must go and see what she's about!
Joy of joys, she's got my lead, it's the time when we go out.
I wonder where we'll go today? I hope it's to the park,
I'll run about and chase my ball, it really is a lark.
It's great to really sniff and snuffle through all the
different scents,
Ho-ho, what's this I've found? My frisbee . . .
I'd wondered where that'd went!
Down to the water, how I love to swim,
Ducks watch out! I'm coming in . . .
The children come over to say 'hello',
But I'm on my way, I've got to go.
The blithesome glee of being out for a walk
Means I've not time to stop and talk.
Home again, a nice big drink. Maybe I'll just have forty-winks!
I'm drifting off, getting ready to run,
Chasing rabbits again, oh such fun!

Joyce Drake

A Boxer's Tale

When I arrived at this house just two years ago,
Not a frightened pup was I, ready for friend and foe,
I announced 'My name is Bhuna and a boxer, I'm here to stay,
But let me warn you Mum and Dad, I'm going to get my way.'

To stop my cries in the night they let me in their bed
As a tiny pup I comfortably squeezed in between their heads,
But a handsome boxer I am today and as big as I can be,
That decision to let me sleep with them is regretted ruefully.

My daily chore is walking Dad, I do it every day,
A harness and a lead attached so he doesn't lose his way.
His confidence grows as we hit the fields, he no longer needs
                                                    his stead,
I've lots of running I need to do so he lets me off my lead.

If I met my doggy mother now I'm sure it would be plain to see,
The loyal, proud, upstanding boxer I've turned out to be.
I remember her last words spoken, as we left the breeder's run,
'The golden rule given to us in life is you must make everything fun!

You've got the pleasure of being a boxer dear, so in everything
                                                    you do,
Live every day like it were your last and to the boxer pride be true,
When you're old and slowing down think back to this day
You'll have done your best if you know you got there doing it
                                                    your way.'

I'm the type to stick to my word, can't let her down you see,
That's why to my mother fair and true I listened carefully,
The golden rule of boxers must be followed day by day,
As I warned them when I arrived, I always get my way!

C L Lowton